ANOTHER
ONE
FOR
BURNING

ANOTHER ONE FOR BURNING

A Collection of Poetry
and Spoken Word

PJ

PHOENIX JAMES

ANOTHER ONE FOR BURNING

First Edition: 2022

ISBN: 978-1-7396788-7-6 (Paperback)
ISBN: 978-1-7396788-8-3 (Ebook)

Cover Photo by Kersten Bower
Cover Artwork & Design by Phoenix James
Book Design & Formatting by Phoenix James

Visit the author's website at www.PhoenixJamesOfficial.com or email him at phoenix@PhoenixJamesOfficial.com

DEDICATION

To your total
And complete
Intellectual freedom

To your right to believe
Whatever you want to
On absolutely any subject

And to express your thoughts
Your opinions and your beliefs
However you deem appropriate

To total and complete freedom
Without any limitation
To the access or production
Of your information and ideas

Regardless of the medium
Of communication you choose.

And to a young free-spirited boy
Whom I knew a long time ago
Before censorship threatened us
I feel you'll approve of this work.

CONTENTS

A NICE WORLD ORDER

Each one help one
We should be nicer to each other
You can never be too nice, can you
If it's two people being nice
I think you can be being too nice
If one's being nice
And the other isn't
Then after a certain point
You're just being a fool or an idiot
But if two people are being nice
It can never be too much
I'll be nicer
I'll outdo you and be nicer the next time
And it just keeps going
And it's just all nice
It's just niceness
That's how the world should be
That should be competition
Who could be the nicest
That should be the new world
How to be nice to people
How to be caring and loving
Who can be most caring, loving and nice
Let that be the competition

I'd like to live in that world
A new amendment
The Nice World Order
That'd be awesome
I'm going to work on it
Will you work with me
To create a nice world order
That's it
Let's get together
And create a nice world order
Rewrite the commandments
Thou shalt be nice to each other
Please and Thank You
Should definitely be on the list
I get told I say thank you too much
You know what I do now
I say it more
I like to express my appreciation
That shows that people
Don't say thank you enough
People are not polite enough
I think it's not that I say it too much
It's that people are not used to it
People are not used to being polite
And saying thank you
So when people make a point of saying it

People will find it uncomfortable
Or unusual or weird
But that's the way it should be
We should express gratitude
I'm liking this
When we get together
We need to sit down with a pen and paper
To put down our points
The new ten commandments
Of the nice world order
This is good
Nice people doing nice things
By being nice to each other
Niceologists
I love it
Why isn't that a thing already
Niceology
The study of Niceology
This is a new thing
This is great.

ABOUT THE RIVER THAMES

I wouldn't want to jump in it
In any weather
Along with the current
I don't think you'd be coming out
With everything else that's in there
I don't think you'd just be coming out wet
And cold
I think you'd come out
With a few more things
You didn't expect to have
I think you'd be asking for trouble
I think you could get dry
And you can get warm
But some things
I don't think you'll be able to get off you
You can get out of your wet clothes
But I don't think you'll be able
To get out of what else you get
While you're in there
Some things that might not be
Coming off your skin so easily
I hear that back in the old days
It's where they used to dump human waste
All the shit and everything

Used to be dumped in the Thames
Along with all the dead bodies
I feel like my skin would just singe off
If I fell in there
No matter how cold it was
Singe off my flesh and everything
Could you imagine
Like falling in toxic waste chemicals
I think you'd suffocate not from drowning
Not from the water going into your body
I think you'd suffocate from the smell of it
Being that close to the water
With your nose to it
I think your nose would singe off as well
I think your flesh
Would just fall off the bones
You'd be a skeleton
The Thames is not appealing
It's not like anyone says
It's a nice day
Let's go dip our feet in the Thames
It's not the first place you think of
I bet those people that were jumping in
In the summer
I bet they never got out again
I heard half of them were drunk

I bet half of them have drowned
Our beautiful London Thames
It looks beautiful at night
And sometimes in the day
If you catch it from the right angle
When it's not looking dirty, grey and brown
I would take the sea in Brighton
Over the Thames any day
I don't know which current is stronger
But if I was going to die
Through the current of either
And I had to choose between
The Thames River and the Brighton sea
I would go for Brighton
Even though the current may be stronger
If I'm going to go
I'm not going in that shit
The Thames.

ANYONE CAN BE PHOTOGENIC

I think what helps
With taking photos
Is that I know
How to take myself
I think when a lot of people
Think they don't look good
In pictures
Is when they don't know
How to take themselves
Or they don't have someone
Who knows how to take them
I think that's a lot to do with it
With looking good in a picture
Or being happy
With how you see yourself
And that's me
I've learned how to take myself
It's practice
It has been practice over time
I know my angles
I know all of that, so that helps
And I think that's important
For people to realise
It's not that they're not photogenic

It's that they don't know
How to take themselves
Or someone else
Doesn't know
How to take them.

BAD NEWS

Stuff that's going on in the news
Bothers me, yes
Because I'm a human being
And I don't like to see anyone come to harm
Or be living in a situation
That's less than they could be
Considering we have so much abundance
In the world
And so many resources
And only certain people
Have access to them
That stuff bothers me
When it doesn't have to be that way
But at the same time
With all of that going on
There's so much beauty in the world as well
There's so many good things
Going on in the world
There's so many things to be happy about
In the world
It's just not being documented in the news
We're seeing mostly the negative things
That are happening in the news
So if you're consuming only that

Or you're consuming the news
As just your window to the world
And what human beings are doing
And living like
Then you're going to find yourself
Looking down on life
And on the behaviour of humankind
When only a portion of it
Is being documented on the news
That annoys me
That only some of it is being shown
And there's a group of people
Only showing what they decide to cover
When it could be balanced out
And the world might seem like a nicer place
And people may be able to make
More informed choices
About the way they live
And the way they see the world
The way they view the world
And the way they feel
When they go out of their houses
Or even if they feel
Like going out of their houses
Because if you watch the news every day
You won't want to leave your house

You're living in fear
That's the part of it that affects me
That I don't like
The fact that I wish
I could give more people that outlook
That it's not all bad
If you watch the news every day
You're not going to feel good in yourself
You're going to think what am I living in
You're not going to feel
That there's any hope for mankind
It's just getting worse and worse and worse
When that's only one portion
That's being documented of how we live
Or how we exist
It's not going to sell newspapers
To say this or that person
Done this amazing great thing
For another human being today
You do every so often
Hear news that someone did a good deed
But the ratio of good news to bad news
That is presented is both disproportionate
And disparaging in comparison
It's more so when someone kills somebody
You're going to hear about that first

You'll always hear it's bad weather today
It's going to be really terrible weather
Huge storm coming
More so than when great sunshine weather
Is on the way
Even when the weather is going to be great
The warnings of soaring heatwaves start
And possible shortages of water due to heat
It's constant fear-mongering
That seems to be the overall aim
The overbearing ratio of the news
Is more towards negativity
With focus on only a fraction of positivity
The minute we switch that box on
Or open that newspaper
We're just pumped full of gloomy news
Once your eyes are looking at it
And your ears are open
You're simply pumped full
Of depressing and discouraging updates
You're receiving five percent positive
Ninety-five percent negative information
That you're receiving and open to
So your outlook
Is going to be mostly negative

When you step outside your door every day
What kind of world does that create
What kind of mindset
What kind of people
Are you in your workplace with
If everyone's stepped out
With a ninety-five percent
Negative outlook on their day
And the people they're around
And the people they have to interact with
On the way to work
On the bus
On the train
And in the office
And then when they get back home
It's interesting how that could change
If more of that percentage was positive
I turned off my TV
And don't put it on for that reason
I want to kind of be more in control
Of the information I absorb
If I watch the news every day
My outlook on life
Is going to be completely different
To what it is now
Which is so far the other way

Ninety-five percent positive
And five percent negative
What the news does
Is take the bad of one thing
And just focuses on that particular area
Not focusing on the other areas
Just that area that's bad
Like an apple
Where you just focus the camera
Zoomed in on the small bad rotten part
And not the rest of it
Which is actually fine
And perfectly good to consume
That's what the news is to me
Like this one big apple, the world
And a small portion of it is rotten
And the news just takes the camera
And points it only at the rotten bit
So no one looking can see
What's beyond the lenses focus point
No one can see
What the camera refuses to show
Nor can they hear
What news the reporters or journalists
Do not report on
They can only see the rotten bit

They can't see that overall
It's still good to eat
This world is good to digest
There's still a lot of good here.

BLAMING OF THE TOOLS

Social media
Another powerful tool
Connects
People say social media is so bad
And the Internet is evil
But it's man-made
It's human beings that are on it
It's not the thing
The tool
Or the vehicle that's bad
It's human beings
There's good and bad in everything
It's the way people use it
They use it for good
Or use it for bad
There's genuine people on it
There's disingenuous people on it
So it's not the thing to be blamed.

BONDING OR BONDAGE

I look at it all as bonding
It's a bonding thing
I feel going to the toilet
In my partner's presence
Or girlfriend or wife
Or whatever
I feel it's bonding
You should be able
To go to the toilet together
In each other's presence
There may come a time when you have to
Okay, maybe not a number two
Maybe not or maybe
But I'm talking about a number one
Just going for wee
I don't think it's a big deal
I think that demonstrates bonding
I think when you're unable to
There's something you haven't let go of
In terms of being free with your partner
There's something you're holding onto
That may be holding you back
From getting closer
I think it's a small thing

I remember one time years ago
With my girlfriend at the time
We were on a bus
And she was ill and she was vomiting
I put my hand to her mouth
To catch the vomit as she was leaning over
It's just something
That I didn't think twice about
I just did it
She thought it was the most amazing thing
But it's nothing to me
It's something I would do
If it's someone you're into
And you're planning to stick around for
I think there's things that should be normal
Or you should try to make normal
If they're not in the beginning
Because you care about the person
I don't think it's something
That needs to be addressed
I don't need to address it
I just do it
I just behave in those ways
The only time I would feel
I need to address it
Is when I feel the other person

Might not get it
Or I get a sense
Of them not being comfortable with it
Or not being fully relaxed
Within themselves or around me
Or things that they feel
They're uncomfortable with
For someone like that
Who has that squeamish thing about them
That's the kind of person
I would feel I need to mention it to
Rather than it just being a normal thing
That just happens naturally
It can make it awkward
But then
I like to make them feel comfortable
By saying I don't mind
Or it's okay
Or that means nothing to me
Especially things like periods
It's really is nothing to me
I don't know what kind of guys
Some of these women are meeting
But to me
A woman on her period
Is a normal thing

It doesn't matter to me
It doesn't make me want to run a mile away
Because you're on your period
Like you can't be around me
I get it in the sense of some people
Having religious beliefs on the subject
But outside of that
I don't see why women think
Oh it's so disgusting
To express that side of themselves
Around the guy
Like they can't even mention the fact
That they're on their period
Or they have to go and change their pad
It's so nothing to me
But maybe it's because most of my life
I've grown up around women
I have sisters
I have a mother
I have grandmothers I've grown up with
So I don't know if it's that
But I just don't take it
As such a big deal
It's so normal
You can't stop it from happening
But people want to stop it from happening

They want to stop nature by shielding it
Sheltering the truth of it away
Covering it up
Oh he can't know, that I'm a woman
That I have to go and do woman things
It's these stories around what they're doing
Trying to cover it up
It's a shame thing
So what if you're on your period
And you need to change your pad
God forbid you've got a spot of blood
On the back of your skirt
Or your trousers
And I have to be the one to tell you about it
I think some people would die
Jesus Christ
It's nothing
It's nature
I've been in that situation a few times
I've had to tell women that on the street
That I don't even know
What am I supposed to do
Go and get a woman to tell you?
Maybe I could do that
To save the person from dying a little bit
From maybe having a heart attack

It's natural and it's normal
I can see where it comes from with guys
That are the other way
Some freaked out guy
He's not going to know what to do
I've got to change my pad
He's going to be the one
To have the heart attack, right?
Six months down the line
When all the real shit starts coming out
The real behaviours
I think it's good to show that stuff
From the door
This is me
I'm real and I'm natural
I wee and I fart
I go to the toilet
I shit
I eat this way
That's another one
Women not wanting to eat in front of guys
I get it
But at the same time
I kind of don't get it
You're human, you eat
I've seen it so many times

As a guy on the receiving
I've seen how many times women say
I can't eat in front of you
Or *I'll only have the salad, I'm not hungry*
And you know they're starving
Jesus, man
It's crazy
I get it but it's still crazy to me
Exhausting is one word for it
I just haven't got the energy
Some people I suppose
Have got the energy
To keep it up
That must be draining
It's like Superwoman or Wonder Woman
She changes from her normal self
To her superhero self
And the keeping up of those two identities
Like Clark Kent being Superman
Having to hide who they really are
That double life
That must be exhausting, man
She eats like a pig by herself
Or with her friends
But when she's with you
She's got to change her whole eating style

She has to eat in small increments
One little tiny bit on the fork
Whereas she would have put two, three
Four times as much on the fork
With her friends or by herself
Or with her family
But being with you as the guy
She's different
One day it comes tumbling down
One day the guy is horrified
When he sees her eating
But she doesn't know he's there
You might be hiding the person
That you think they won't like
And that may be the person they like
More than the person you're presenting
Now there's a thing
They may fall more in love
With the person you really are
Than the person you're putting forth.

CAMERAS, HAIR & CUSTOMER CARE

I'm in Victoria right now
Victoria Station
Having a double espresso
From Costa Coffee
I've just come off the train
So I'm just chilling out
On this wonderful evening
I inspired a friend to get himself a camera
I think that not only him but everyone
Should have a camera of some kind
We all of course already own one now
With the advent of smart phones
But I think we should always use them
Or even better have a dedicated camera
Specifically for taking pictures and video
Even if you don't have a smart phone
I think everyone should have a camera
I recommend it
I recommend, I recommend, I recommend
Documenting, document, document
All aspects of your life
Or at least be prepared to
Always have it there
Because you can't go wrong

Having a little compact camera
In your pocket when you're ready to go
Or when you need to document
Or catch something wherever you are
My mum was telling me the other day
That she had an ice cream
When she was away recently
And in the bottom of the ice cream pot
When she'd reached the end
There was a hair
She told the staff about the hair
And they were giving her a hard time
Talking about the hair
Examining and looking at it
Passing it around to each other
Trying to establish who it belonged to
Claiming that the hair in question
Didn't belong to anyone who served her
It was all just completely ridiculous
They were also trying to claim
That she'd eaten it already
So therefore there's nothing they could do
All of which should never have happened
They should have just rectified it right away
From a customer complaint point of view
But they continued refusing responsibility

Eventually she was given her money back
It was just this whole thing
And I was thinking to myself
If that was me, these days
Because I always have a camera
I would be documenting all of that fiasco
You wouldn't get away with that rubbish
Basically, I would have filmed the evidence
That the hair was in there in the first place
I'm often always filming in food places
And taking pictures of my food anyway
So it would've been there documented
Then I would have gone to them politely
And explained what happened
Expecting them to swiftly resolve the issue
Considering I am a paying customer
Who has chosen to use their service
I wouldn't let any place just dismiss me
I'd protest just as my mum did that day
I wouldn't let any place at any time
Get away with that behaviour now
Don't be mistreating your customers
That's one of the purposes and benefits
Of having the ability to document
And capture things like that on camera
Because people need to know

What is right and what is wrong
If a customer is complaining
That they've found a hair in their food
They don't want to hear staff saying
Oh it's not my hair in the bottom of there
I wasn't the one who served you
Anyway, there's nothing we can do now
You've eaten more than half of it already
No, do the right thing
Apologise and rectify the situation
To the best of your ability
You're not being accountable, man
It's just not acceptable
That's the good thing
About having an online platform as well
You know, to make people accountable
All of us have a platform now
To make people accountable for things
And it should be used as such
Especially things like that
I asked my friend what camera
He's planning to get for himself
He says he'll go with the Canon G7X
Either the Mark I, II or III
It's a really good camera
I swear by my Mark I

If you can call it that
I think the Marks
Are only called that after the original
To establish what model version it is
I'm a proud owner of the first version
And it's still going strong.

CONFIDENCE THAT MONEY BRINGS

When you have the money
When your finances
Are sorted out a little bit
You're a bit more confident
About spending money
As in who pays for the bill
You're a bit more self assured
It gives you confidence
That you don't have to worry
Are we going to split this bill
Is she going to make me pay for all of it
You're a bit more at ease
I don't need to worry
You can relax a bit
You're a bit more confident to say
Let's go out on a date
Because you're not worried
About the fact
That you have to spend money
Whether she's paying half or not
Whether she's splitting the bill
I won't have to worry about that
It won't bother me
I won't be sitting at the table sweating

For the entire meal
Like how much is it going to come to
What kind of drink will she say she wants
How much is it going to cost
Having a bit of money
You're a bit more confident
Let's go for a date, you choose the place
It gives you that freedom
It makes you puff your chest out a little bit
You're not thinking, this is your gas money
The amount of drinks she's ordering
Like, fuck
This is really going to eat into my pocket
My monthly cheque
You're not worried so much.

COULD HAPPILY STAY IN BED LONGER

Good morning
Happy Saturday to you
One of those Saturdays
I could quite gladly
Stay in my bed
And sleep
Not wake up at 5:30 a.m
Happily snooze till noon
But I must awaken
I must arise
I must get myself up
And out the door
People, if you're having a lie-in
This morning
This Saturday morning
This early Saturday morning
I envy you
This is one morning
I could quite happily
Stay in bed
And sleep
But got to get up.

DEAL BREAKER ON A FIRST DATE

On a first date
What would be a deal breaker
For me, one
Someone who is at the table
On our date
Incessantly communicating on their phone
More than they're communicating with me
Who's actually in front of them
On a first date, no
Pretty much shouldn't do that on any date
But on a first date
For me
That would be a deal breaker
For me, two
Excessive makeup would kind of put me off
Makeup is fine
No problem with makeup
But excessive makeup
Makeup like cake mix, no
Deal breaker
And three
Would be a woman
Who does not want to pay for our entire bill
For the evening

Deal breaker
No, I'm joking about that one
But the other two
Yeah, kind of deal breakers for me
Especially the first one
And probably especially the second one
In regards to the makeup
I just think about
How many of my good clothes
Will be ruined by excessive makeup
I'm speaking from experience here
And when I say deal breaker
I mean, no second date
I'm out
See ya
What's a first date deal breaker
For you?

EXPLORING THE FANTASY

Some people just like parts of you
But not you
They like parts
But not the whole of you
And they don't like the whole of you
Because the parts they're not interested in
Are a part of that whole
And it becomes a conflict
With the parts they do like
Because they have to accept with it
Parts that they don't want to have
Sometimes it's not always sex
Often it just may be
Something that you're associated with
That they feel
Once they're associated with you
They'll be associated with that thing
But they don't want the other stuff
That comes with it
Happens a lot with women actually
When they want to be associated with a guy
But the guy who's associated with that thing
That she's trying to get next to
Is only interested in her for sex

So she has to deal with his sexual advances
But she's not interested in him for sex
She's interested in
Whatever being associated with him
Will get her
So sometimes it's not sex
Sometimes it's some attachment
To something that guy or that person has
And vice versa
It's not just with men
But with women as well
Women sometimes want to get with a guy
But he's not looking at her that way
He sees an opportunity
To maybe connect with someone else
That she's associated with
And it goes around and around
But other times it's often sex
Sex is the thing
But they don't want the other parts
Of that person
That person may be really good in bed
Or they really have a sexual attraction
To that person
But they're not interested
When they talk about something else

They may really be into graphic novels
And model aeroplanes
Or train sets
Or bird-watching
Something that they're really not into
But they like the sex
However they don't want
To deal with other parts of that person
They don't really want the person
It's just the fantasy they want to play out
And that only goes so far
Once they've explored that fantasy
They don't want anymore
They're off
I've also been in that situation
I've been the one
Who wanted to play out the fantasy
And then once the fantasy was explored
I wasn't that interested anymore
I've been a victim of that
And I've been a perpetrator of that
Who feels it knows it, right?
We can talk about it
When we know it
When we've either
Seen it happen to someone else

Or ourselves
Or we've been the ones
Who have been doing it
For me it's both
I can hold my hands up
And say it's both
Rather than suffer with the curiosity
Of not knowing
You kind of want to play it out
You want to play out the fantasy
And see where it goes and explore it
Rather than live with the not knowing
The regret of not knowing
Or trying to play it out
People want to explore
They don't want to not know.

FAVOURITE SEXUAL POSITION

I don't know
If I have a favourite sexual position
I kind of like a bit of everything
I like spooning
I like laying on her back
I don't know what you call that
I guess you could call that forking
Doggy style
I like them all
I like cowgirl
Then reverse cowgirl
Missionary is nice
I like missionary a lot
All of them
I like her feet on my shoulders
I like everything, man
I'm not turning down anything
I can't think of a position I don't like
So I guess, I must like everything
I don't know if that's everybody
But I like everything
If it's going, I'll have it
Yeah there's nothing I don't like
I guess the question is

What is my favourite
I like the closeness of missionary
It's really like one big hug
With more to it
I like that because it's very lovey-dovey
Or it should be
I like missionary a lot because
You can kiss as well at the same time
And you can be at each other's faces
You can use your mouth
And express yourself with that person
Kissing their face
Kissing their chests
Kissing their forehead
Kissing their ears and neck
It's just that whole
Affectionate, kissy, kissy type lovemaking
You can really do that
When you're face to face in missionary
So I guess that's one of the appeals for me
And the closeness
It's like you're hugging almost
It's that whole lovey-dovey type lovemaking
I think missionary is a big one
Because I'm just a lovey-dovey type
Romantic type guy

But I like the others too
As I said, I like forking
I'm calling it forking
That's my name for it
When you lie on the person's back
If there's spooning
When you're on the side
Then it has to be forking
Like putting two folks together
It makes sense
Missionary is standard
To my knowledge
It's considered the standard one
I think it depends on the person
Whether or not they consider it boring
I think if it was only missionary
I'd find it boring
But combined with other things
It's great
But then again there's times
When I only want to do that
Because I just like that whole feeling
Of that that closeness
You really feel like you're making love
When you're having a proper
Good old missionary

Yeah, that's when you really feel
That you're making love, man
In my opinion
For example
What other position
Are you that close and intimate
With the person
In terms of legs wrapped around
Embraced
Close
I think that's where a woman is most open
In missionary
Men are the givers
And women are the receivers
I feel that's where a women
Is most open to a man
When she's in a missionary position
In my humble opinion
I think so
And that's what also makes it quite intimate
The fact that she's so open
And he's there to give
They're both in a position of closeness.

FUTURE TV ADDICT & BINGE-WATCHER

So many things I want to watch
I hope to watch them in my old age
At some point
When I've got nothing else to do
But sit down and watch telly
And old programs
Oh this is what everyone was talking about
This show is amazing
In forty years time
I'll be hooked on Breaking Bad
In thirty or forty years time
I'll be asking, have you seen The Wire
When there's flying cars outside
After the robots have killed us
I'll be asking, who's seen Game of Thrones
It's amazing
I love the thought that with all these shows
That are now there
You can go back and watch them
They're recorded
I could go back and watch them in ten years
If I wanted to
I love that
It's kind of cool

Because I think that's the only time
I'm really going get to sit down
And watch all of these box sets
And all these Netflix shows
That everyone rants about
I'm too busy, man
I haven't got time
To sit down and watch them now
I've got shit to do
When I haven't got shit to do
When I'm maybe immobile
I'll sit down
And binge on all these TV shows
When I've got time to sit down and wonder
Where all the time in my life went
I can do it then
Right now
I'm trying to use the time.

GETTING SMART

I just saw the police
Chasing somebody down the street
They're searching some boys
I think one of them must have just ran
Just bolted
That happens a lot on that road
One girl I know
Had her phone stolen on that road
She was coming out of the cinema
And she was about to cross the road
Looking down at her phone
She was on the edge pavement
Waiting for gap in the traffic
So she could cross
And then a motorbike came
As if out of nowhere
And just swiped her phone out of her hand
I'm guilty of it too
You just get in a habit
Of looking down at your phone
When you're walking
You get to the side of a road
You need to cross
And you're not really thinking

That someone's going to ride past
On a motorbike
And swipe your phone out of your hand
But I've become more aware of it now
Just because of some of the kind of people
I've been around lately
And some of the stories I hear
It's definitely made me more aware
Of standing at the roadside
With my phone in my hands
But to be fair
I'm not really using a smart phone
At the moment
So that's brought risk down a little bit
Which is a benefit
To not having a smartphone
You're not constantly looking at your screen
I much prefer it for the battery life
It's so much better
My Nokia, man
It's just so trusty
It hasn't run out of juice
Usually your phone will run down
To nothing
And you have to start charging it
This phone doesn't run down like that

I could speak to you for a good few hours
Before it even showed a sign of moving
I love it
When my Galaxy Note 3 started getting old
It started underperforming, so to speak
I got a new battery and it's just so old
That it just didn't hold its charge anymore
So I had to use an external charger
A lot more often
And then that ended up not working
So I was kind of without a phone
Unless I was plugged into a mains supply
So that was just troublesome
I love not having a smart phone right now
Because I'm not constantly
Looking at my screen just out of boredom
What is so amazing as well
Is that I've seen places I frequent every day
But I've never really seen those places
I'm seeing them now
Because my head is up
It's amazing
I've been passing this place ten years
And I've never seen it before
We miss so much
It's crazy.

HER GAY BEST FRIEND

One thing I don't understand
Or I'm yet to comprehend
Or someone has yet to explain to me
Why when a guy is looking at a girl
Who is with a guy
Does the guy with the girl get upset
With the guy or get angry
Because the guy is looking at the girl
Okay so to be clear
There's a girl and a guy together
And there's another guy
Who's nothing to do with them
He just looking at the girl
And the guy is getting upset
With the guy who is looking at her
Let's not put her in the picture yet
Let's just say he's getting upset
With the guy that's looking at her
I've never understood it really
I get it
People for whatever reasons get upset
Because someone's looking at their girl
They feel disrespected
It's the possessive thing

Territorial

I can understand that

Okay, let's put me in the picture

Let's say I'm looking at a girl

And she's with a guy

I don't know what their relationship is

I've just seen a girl that I like the look of

So I'm looking at her

Now unless you're holding hands

Or you're kissing on each other

Both being affectionate in that way

Or it's somehow made apparent

That you're together

I don't see that I'm doing anything wrong

Obviously the guy may feel that I am

But I feel, in his mind

He should be more concerned with

What is the girl doing

Is she responding to these advances

I've always thought, if it's me

That I should be looking at

What my girl is doing

Is she responding to this guy looking

What is she doing

That's the more important thing

Because guys

Are going to do what guys are going to do
They're going to look at girls
That's what guys do
I've been in situations
Where I've been looking at a girl
And didn't even realise she's with a guy
And then I have to catch myself
And I realise there's this guy
His eyes beaming through me
Ready to kill me
In that moment it dawns on me
But prior to that
I didn't even realise
That there's a guy with her
Until after the event
After I get this energy
Of what are you looking at
That's only when I realise, oh shit
I'm out of place here
And I get it
I find it disrespectful
When there's a couple
And then the guy's looking at the girl
When he can clearly see their a couple
I think that's disrespectful
I would try not to do that

I've been in those situations
On both sides
But I never get angry with the guy
I never think I want to punch this guy
You can clearly see I'm with this girl
We're hugging
We're kissing
I never get angry at the guy
Or want to have words with the guy
I know what guys are like
I'm a guy
I'd more be interested in seeing
What my girl is doing
While that's going with him
I'm looking at her
My eyes are on her
I'm not on him
I don't care what he's doing
I'm not with him
He could be licking his lips at her
He could be calling her over
He could be signalling to his phone
As if to say to her, can I get your number
As long as she's not entertaining it
I don't really care what he's doing
As long as she's showing him

In her actions
That she's with me
And that's if she recognises
That he's even there
If she even acknowledges him at all
I'd be more focused on what she's doing
I don't get this idea
Of like getting angry with the guy
It's the same thing you probably did
To get the girl in the first place
Maybe
And if it's a prolonged thing
He keeps on doing it
He's still looking at her
Like wait a minute
I've gone to the toilet
I've come back
And he's still looking
I'd have to be like, okay
What's she doing
Forget him
Is she looking back at him
Is there like an exchanging of glances
I'm more interested in that
That's what I'm focused on
Because that's the person I'm with

And vice-versa
For the woman who's with a guy
Who's seen a girl looking at him
Same thing
She should be focused on
What her man is doing
Is he entertaining this girl
Who is making advances with her eyes
Who's trying to show her bum a bit more
Because the guy is there
Hoping that he'll take a look and be excited
She should be looking at what he's doing
Is he responding to it
But what happens is
People tend to get angry at the person
The random stranger who's drooling
Whom they have no concern with
Like I said, I get it
I think they're angry at the wrong person
Or getting angry unnecessarily
It comes from feeling disrespected
It comes from seeing the opposite sex
Looking at your partner
It's a disrespecting thing
I see it as disrespectful
When someone does that

When they clearly can see
You're in a relationship with someone
Or you're clearly together in that way
I've been in situations where I've said
To the guy that's with the girl I'm looking at
Well, I thought you fancied me
I didn't know this was your girlfriend
I just saw you staring at me all the time
I didn't know you were mad at me
Because I was looking at your girl
I'm looking at the girl with you
Because she's attractive
I didn't know it was your girlfriend
I thought you were her gay best friend
Yeah, I thought you fancied me
I thought you were interested in me
While I'm interested in your girl
That's what I thought
I didn't know, I'm sorry
I apologise
I thought you were fancying me
While I'm fancying her
What are you staring at me for
Why are you making eyes at me
Look at your girl
What's she doing

It's crazy to me
That's what girls and guys do
If they have a level of respect or not
They are naturally
Attracted to the opposite sex
If they're taking it a bit further
Where they see that you're with someone
And they don't care
They're just looking anyway
I'm not even interested
I want to know
Is my partner, the person I'm with
Are they responding
That's my main focus
I'm not coming to talk to you
To get in an argument with you
It's a waste of my energy
I know you're interested in my girl
I know that, I can see that
I get that she's attractive
You can't help your eyes
I understand
Normal
It's what is she going to do about that
That's what I'm interested in
How is she responding to that

That's what I should be focused on
Because again, men are going to do
What men are going to do
And women, they're going to do
What women are going to do
These gay best friends
Just want to be looking at me
What can I do
I can't get mad at the guy
If he fancies men, he fancies men
I can't be mad
That's what he's into
I just have to let him know
I'm looking at her
I'm not looking at you
Because I'm looking at a girl
And this guy is just staring, staring, staring.

I LIKE PROGRESS MORE THAN SLEEP

Good morning
Been up since 4 a.m
It's 5 a.m now
So I've been up an hour
Gathering my thoughts
It's a good time to be awake
When the earth is still relatively still
And one can think
Before the busy world awakes
And everything is moving
And in motion
I like to exist in the stillness
I like to be awake in it
And have that space
To let my thoughts travel
Travel beyond the busy city
Or before the busy city
When the earth is still relatively quiet
Uninterrupted thoughts can travel
Just thinking time basically
I like it
It's all very quiet
Even at this time
Even the 5 a.m

It's just relatively still
At least where I am
Due to get up shortly
And start my day
This is actually a lie-in for me
That's funny
A lot of the time I'm up at 3 a.m
To seize the day
It's interesting what motivates you
To get up
Or wake up
And be productive
When there's no one telling you to
When there's no one forcing you to
When there's no boss
Breathing down your neck
To arrive at his workplace for this time
Or that time
It definitely feels
Like you're doing something pretty amazing
When you can do that yourself
When you don't have to
It definitely adds to your day
Those extra hours that you sacrifice
By getting up early
Before the rest of the world

Makes such a difference
When by 10 a.m
You've already pretty much
Completed your day
And the rest of the day is yours
To do whatever you want to do
That's a nice place to be at
So I enjoy waking up at 3 a.m
Even when people would say
You don't have to
I like it
Because I just like progress
More than I like sleep
And so I will sacrifice sleeping in
When I don't have to
I don't have to sleep in
It's a choice
I can wake up
And do what I have to do
And it feels good
It feels majorly good
I'm off to start my day
Enjoy yours.

JUST WITNESSED A ROBBERY

I witnessed a robbery this morning
From a jewellery shop
I was a little stunned by it
A guy ran out with jewellery in his hand
Right past me
The woman in the shop screamed out
While this was happening
The guy is running across the street
Getting away with the bunch of jewellery
This other guy also exits the jewellery shop
After the first one
And a few people are holding him
From also getting away
Including a man I recognised
Who works in the shop next door
This is all because the woman is saying
That the second guy
Held the door
For the first guy who ran away
So they were holding onto him
He was trying to tell them
That he had nothing to do with the first guy
As an outsider looking at the situation
I think they were both together

But he's insisting that they weren't
And that he was in the store by himself
And the lady is protesting profusely
That he is the other guy's accomplice
I've never witnessed anything like that
So close up
I'm trying to think of a time
Where I've actually seen
A robbery like that in person
I don't think so
Not that I can remember
Maybe I've forgotten
But definitely not in recent years
I'm saying in recent years
But I don't think I've ever witnessed
Anything like that before
Apart from watching it on TV
When they show those programs
And they show the real CCTV footage
Of how the criminals robbed the place
I've seen that stuff
But this was up live in my face
I literally felt the wind
From the guy who ran past me
That's why I say I was stunned for a second
It's just like part movie

And part *is this real* in my head
I was just there taken aback for a second
I watched him run clean across the street
Towards the churchyard
And then another guy ran out
Chasing after him
While they held this other guy
By the shop door
I not sure if was he armed
He could have been
But I remember him with the gloves on
And the shiny jewellery in his hand
As he was running away
It felt like he did a grab and run
Because you heard the lady scream out
Then you see this other guy
Kind of in the doorway
And them holding him
It couldn't have been no more
Than sixty seconds
That the whole thing took place
They were just holding the guy
Deciding what to do with him
I had an appointment so I had to leave
It was a lot
I've never seen anything like that

The first guy literally would've run me over
If I was any closer to him
He's just robbed somewhere
He's trying to get away
So if you're in his way
You're going to get run over
I'm lucky that I wasn't any closer to him
I don't know if he had a getaway vehicle
He might've been running to it
But I feel that he came on foot
And was leaving on foot
I don't think he actually rode there
It was one of those smash and grab things
Though I don't think he smashed anything
Just a grab and run
I witnessed a real live robbery
In front of my face
I am a witness
Except I couldn't tell you
What the first guy looked like
Because he ran so fast past me
And by the time I was looking at him
It was his back towards me running away
So I couldn't give a description of him at all
The most I could describe
Is maybe his height

But I might even get that wrong
Because he was moving
At such a speed past me
At that moment
That the only other person I could describe
Is the person who they held
Which everyone saw
Because they held him there
And I left and they were still holding him
So everyone saw him
He's probably on the CCTV camera anyway
So there'd be no need for me
To describe what he looked like
Everyone obviously got his description
The other guy was clean gone
With a fistful of jewellery
I don't know what he had
Or how much it cost
But he was off
It was an eventful moment
I didn't stick around that long
I was long gone before any police came
To ask anyone about witness statements
The guy was probably still running
I left while they were likely still chasing him
Wherever they were chasing him

A real life robbery, man
A real life jewellery shop grab and run.

KEEPING OUT OF TROUBLE

I don't like breaks
Breaks are not good for me
If there's a break coming up
I've got to find something to do
The reason I'm always active
And doing stuff
Is because it keeps me out of trouble
I say that as a joke
But it really does keep me out of trouble
Because I don't get to dwell
On things that will put me
In a negative state
Or a state that's not so good to be in
So I keep myself busy
To keep my mind right
And stay focused on something
That is not going to make me depressed
Or get me in a depressed state
And depression is never good
I keep myself busy, man
People laugh when I say
I've been keeping out of trouble
And they don't really get it
When I say it

They just think it's just a funny joke
And it is a funny joke
But it's real at the same time
There's no break
I don't like breaks
I like to be busy
I just like working
I like creating
I like being busy
I don't like it
When there's nothing going on
That's when I get frustrated
People say you're always busy
I'm always busy because
I make sure that I'm always busy
People think I work too hard
But trust me
It's better I'm doing that
Than anything else
Believe me
It's better I don't have time
To think about anything
That I don't have that space to dwell
It's much better for me
And those around me
Some people don't get it

The break is not the good thing
That's the wrong thing
You find things to fill your time with
When it's like that
On purpose
You keep sane
I'm keeping myself sane
By keeping myself busy
And active
Keeping out of trouble.

MAYBE NEW YORK

Where would I live
If I didn't live in London
So many places to be honest
I think I could live in New York
I like the energy
I just feel I would be at home there
In London
I pretty much can get anything I want
And get to anywhere I want at any time
And I feel New York would just be that
But scaled up a bit more
That same thing but ramped up a bit
I feel like I could thrive there
Even more so than in London
So New York would be my first choice
For another place to live other than London
If I had to choose.

MY DARLING JAMES

I was so shy
I left you all to it
You did well
Going up there and singing that
We were all supposed to go up
And sing the song together
'I Wanna Sex You Up'
Everybody's favourite song at the time
And I chickened out
I didn't know you also sang a song for me
I had no idea
How do I not know anything about this
What cloud was I on
That I don't even know this
I think I was so naive in school
You're saying that the three of you
Made up a different song
Specifically for me
And sung it
In front of the whole assembly
Wow
When does this happen
Why do I not remember this
Why did the three of you

Get up on stage
In front of the whole assembly
And sing a song dedicated to one pupil
What was that about
Clearly you all liked me
I was the "hot boy on campus"
That's hilarious
And you sung it in front of everyone
That is crazy
You all actually penned a song
Specifically for me
I can't even imagine you all
Sitting down
Writing this song
Rehearsing it
Choosing who's going to sing what
I would've loved to watch that on video
I don't know how I don't remember it
I was obviously present
At least I think I would've been
I remember you all getting up there
Singing "I Wanna Sex You Up"
And I was supposed to sing with you
But as I said, I chickened out
So that must've been a different time
A song dedicated to me called

"My Darling James" Wow
Do you know what?
If you all did an adult version now
I'd love you all forever
That would be so awesome
You have to do it now
You know that, right
Since you're all in contact still
I think I was very naive back then
Because I don't know what was going on
I don't know how I missed this
Three females get up on stage
And sing a song dedicated specifically to me
And it's not the biggest thing
Of my whole year
I don't know how this could be
"My Darling James"
Wow, what a title
I just don't remember it
I must have missed it or something
That you remember the words even now
That's hilarious
You all had a crush on me
I'm feeling like I missed out
I'm feeling like I missed the boat
This is like a revelation

That I had no idea about
I must have misheard
Or had not been present
Or not paying attention
I don't know what happened
But you say I was definitely there
That's amazing.

ON HAVING BABIES LATER IN LIFE

I think if you can
And it's not going to be a complication
To yourself or to your life
And you can bring life into the world
Healthily and happily
Why not
Whatever your age
A friend of mine
His mother had him at fifty
And he's here alive today
Healthy and strong
And we're friends
He's gone on to get married
And have two children
It's great
If his mother decided not to have him
Because of her age
Then he would not be here
To share his life with someone else
And then to create offspring of his own
It's beautiful
I was at his wedding
It's a beautiful thing
That's my take on it

There are of course other factors
That obviously
Would need to be taken into consideration
But for me personally
I think it's a beautiful thing
There's a lot of things
That may make it not a good idea
People often talk about other people
Or themselves being too old and unable
To run around and play with their children
If they were to have them past a certain age
As a reason why no-one should do it
Which is to be taken into account as well
Because by the time they're twenty
If you were fifty at their birth
You're going to be seventy years old
So I get that way of thinking
But I think it's a beautiful thing
I think it's a great thing
That people are able to do that
To still conceive at a certain age
To have a baby
To bring life into the world
I also like to think
That no child will grow up to say
That they wish

Their old parents
Who gave birth to them or adopted them
Much later in life
Decided not to have me.

ON VISITING EGYPT & THE PYRAMIDS

I went to Egypt in 1999
And saw the pyramids
I went to Karnak, Aswan and Kom Ombo
Edfu, Valley of the Kings and Luxor
I stayed in Cairo
It was a really good experience
I definitely recommend it
For anyone's bucket list
I think it's probably
On most people's bucket list
To visit Egypt and the pyramids
I went there two weeks after
Some British tourists were killed
It was a pretty hot situation
At the time that I went
But I was determined to go
And just went there
What I did which was a really good idea
Is I went by camel and horse
Across the desert
At 4 o'clock in the morning
I'm not sure exactly what time I arrived
But it was well before all the excursions
And other visiting tourists were coming

To visit the pyramids
So I had the whole place for myself
For the period that I was there
I got to go around all the pyramids
And climb halfway up the outside of one
It's pretty awesome
I could've climbed to the top
But I chickened out
It's quite high up
It's really great to experience
I recommend going early
In the early hours of the morning if you can
Across the desert
Going to see it all that way
Seeing the sunrise come up over the Sahara
It's so beautiful
Definitely one of the best things I've done
When crossing the desert the night I did
I was thinking to myself
I'm in the middle of the vast desert
In a strange country
I don't know anyone
I'm going across the desert with strangers
In the cold and pitch black dead of night
Can't even see my hands
Anything could happen to me

At that very moment
I looked up into the dark sky
And I saw a shooting star go across the sky
This was for me
Confirmation at that moment
That everything was okay
That I was doing the right thing
I was on the right path
I don't remember making a wish
But it definitely was reassurance
You're safe
This is where you're supposed to be
It was like a sign
After that everything was great
It was confirmation
Especially with the horrific events
That had taken place within the country
Two weeks earlier
And that were still fresh around that time
They're definitely a sight to behold.

PERFECT FIRST DATE BUT THIS PUT ME OFF

We were on a date
In a nice little bar having a few drinks
Things were going really nice
We'd spent most of the day
In each others company
Good conversation between us
And what felt like a great vibe
Then all of a sudden out of nowhere
She said she didn't want anything
To go any further with me
Until she felt the size of my manhood
That's right
She wanted to feel the size of my dick
Before we went any further
She was adamant on knowing the size
Said she didn't want to waste her time
That she'd been let down before
And ended up disappointed
And she needed to know right now
Before we continued the possibility
Of exploring things going deeper
Excuse the pun
But yeah
That just put me off, man.

PLANNING AN EARLY NIGHT

Planning an early night tonight
Let's see what transpires
Let's see if the gods are on my side
Or if they're laughing in the distance
I can almost hear them laughing now
Cackling away
Early night
It's the weekend
Wahahahaha
He's so crazy
Hahahaha
I can just hear them now
But hoping for an early night
I think I need it
I have an early start tomorrow
A really early start
Travelling
So yeah
Rest time
Time to get a rest for the road
As they say
Let's see what happens.

SEX TAPE & TWO MIDNIGHT COFFEES

Two coffees at midnight
Probably wasn't a great idea
Looking back
In hindsight
My mind
Is just bouncing off the walls
Brain completely wired
Sleeping is a myth right now
I did see a good movie tonight though
Sex Tape
Very funny
Very entertaining
Enjoyed that
Coffee brain
I am wide awake
Considering the amount of time
I've been awake already
I should be way tired now
And ready for sleep
But I'm not
I am wide awake
Laying in the dark
Staring into darkness
Trying to sleep

But that isn't going to work for now
That's for sure
I'll sleep eventually
Sometime before the end of the year
If how I'm feeling now is anything to go by
I do not feel tired at all
It's the morning of Christmas Eve
I wonder what everyone's doing today
The last-minute Christmas shopping
Wrapping presents
Tying up Christmas stockings
Above the fireplace
Last-minute decorations
Arrangements around the tree
Presents
Food of course
Christmas dinner preparations
Yeah, Christmas
What does Christmas mean
What it means for me right now
Is this flu bug that's going around
I've managed to pick up somehow
Which is unusual
I don't usually get ill at all
But here we are
Riding the bug, you could say

One thing, when I do get ill
Or I do pick up a bug or anything like that
It doesn't stay long in my system at all
My immune system is pretty good that way
It seems to fight things off pretty quickly
Long may it last
I think that's why my eyes hurt a little bit
The flu symptoms are crazy
And all over the place
I'm not too bad, I'm all right
I had a bit of an upset stomach yesterday
I think that was the onset of it
The beginning
Now it's just in the throat a little bit
Tickly throat, scratchy throat
Throat gets a bit dry
Runny nose
And other flu-like symptoms
But I'm good
I feel like I'm on the road to recovery
But I'm expecting a hundred percent
Right away
I'm sure I'll be still blowing my nose
Well into the evening of Christmas
I sound a little blocked up
Definitely different from usual

84

A bug has attacked me
A frightful bug
It's Christmas time again
I'm so wide awake
I had a pretty chilled evening
Night you could say
I saw another movie
After watching Sex Tape
A really great Christmas movie
It was bit like Groundhog Day
This guy just kept on waking up
At the same place
Because his son made this wish
Wishing it could be Christmas every day
And so he kept on waking up
Reliving the same day
Over and over again
It's pretty cool
He was visiting his son that Christmas
He and his wife were divorced
Living separate lives and stuff
She'd moved on
She had a boyfriend
And the whole family dynamics around that
It was a cool film
It was a good film, I enjoyed it

That probably hasn't told you much
It would've probably been easier
If I just told you the title
But I just don't remember it
It's just a great film
Just a great romantic happy ending film
I had an entertaining evening
Watching movies basically
Coughing again
I'm ill, I'm ill
And can't sleep
I'm just getting flashbacks of the film
Sorry I can't remember the name of it
There's been some workmen
Working on the house next door
They're doing a loft conversion
Every day without fail
They're just working away
The breaking your sleep type working away
When you're sleeping
And you just wake up to hammering
And drilling
And shouting
You know how it is
When workmen are working
I am so glad

They appear to have gone home
For Christmas
Gone home to their families
And doing the Christmas thing
So it was pretty great
To wake up this morning
And not have to hear them
To not have my sleep broken
By the sound of workmen
Working away
Builders, yes
That's what they're called
Builders
Building away on the roof there
It's quite a nice feeling
And it's going to be equally
A nice feeling
Not waking up to that noise today
Of course, that's after
I eventually go to sleep and wake up
There'll be no builders
Because they're off
Doing their family Christmas time
No doubt enjoying their Christmas holidays
And travelling
And buying presents

And doing whatever builders do
When they're off for Christmas
So yeah, looking forward to that
Not having to have that be a thing
So it's all good
I'm seeing flashbacks
Of the Sex Tape movie now
It was pretty good
Enjoyed that immensely
If you haven't seen it, you should
It's very fun and sexy and entertaining
Like imagine you worst nightmare
If you ever made a sex tape
It just leaked basically
And got out there
So it's basically all about that
And them trying to track down
All of the places it had leaked to
And to stop it and that whole journey
It was really fun, I enjoyed that
I do love a good old sex tape
So I've just got flashbacks
Of the movies I caught this evening
Playing back in my head
I'm just so wired
So coffee wired

Coffee high
I don't know what I was thinking
Yeah great, have two coffees
Around midnight
That's a great idea
That was not a great idea
Maybe I'll just talk myself to sleep
Wishing I could sleep myself to sleep
That'd be good
I can watch replays
Of the movies I've watched this evening
In my head until then
Until sleep eventually takes me
What's not fun is when you want to sleep
But you can't
You really want to sleep
But you're not tired
That's a good thing in a lot of cases
In a lot of cases I've enjoyed that
Because I've wanted to be awake
To do things
And being awake and alert has been great
Even though I know I should be sleeping
I've enjoyed not feeling tired
So I could get things done
And that's kind of what I was going with

The having the coffee thing
But I think two was overdoing it
That's the real story
I was doing a few bits
And I had one coffee too many
I think I was just enjoying the taste of it
And just said, I'll have another one
And that was just a not good idea
Now I'm too wired
Wired is good
When you're too wired
You just can't sleep
After you've long done what you had to do
Now it's time to sleep, I cannot sleep
So here I am
Talking to you
Thank you for joining me
Ramblings of a midnight coffee man.

SPLIT MY PANTS

It's just one of those things
That kind of affects your day
I've got a big rip in a section of my pants
A big tear
A big rip in the crotch of my jeans
I think it's just general wear and tear
Or maybe I've just put on weight
I don't know what it is
They've just split
What can I say
Maybe I've been too much on the cakes
I don't know
But they shall be going to retire
Once I take them off
But for now
I have to deal with the fact
That I'm walking around
With a massive tear
That is visible if you're paying attention
If you look
You can see
My colourful underwear underneath
If I look in a mirror from the back
I can actually see them

I see the tear without bending over
It's a bit of a dilemma right now
And obviously, if I sit with my legs open
You can see it from the front
I'm not a far distance from home
But it's about the time of going home
Getting changed and coming out again
It'll take me an hour
To go from where I am at now
To go home and back and get changed
It's time out of my day
It's not important enough
For me to take an hour journey
Back and forth to do that
It's not that important
But it has added something to my day
That I didn't anticipate
Being a part of my day.

STRIPPING, SHEDDING AND SHARING

I want as much as possible
I can't get enough
The more I can strip bare
And show myself
Is the closer I'm going to get
To the person for me
They're going to know me
It's going to be out there
And when I meet someone
I'm not going to be afraid of anything
Because everything is out there
In the world already
On the internet or wherever
So when I meet someone
I can be honest
Because I've shed all of that shit
That we hold on to
That's what I feel
I feel like it's good
The more that's out there
Because I'm free then
So when they see me
They're dealing with a real person
A person who's not afraid

To be their self
Because they're not hiding any skeletons
They've got them all out there
That's how I see it
I think we all go through this place
Where we are
Things happen to us in our lives
And experiences
And then we just have this thing
Of worrying about what other people think
About who we are
And what we've experienced
And are they're going to like us
And all of our scars
All of our internal scars
How they're going to make us look
I think we all have that
I think it's good when we can let go of it
When we learn to let go of it
Not everyone does
Some hold onto that shit forever
We all have it
But I think some of us learn to let go
And some people are in such a way
That it doesn't affect them
They already enter into life

Not caring what people think
Just because of nurture
Because of the way
They've been put through life
Parenting or whatever it might be
They just come out the other side
Not giving a fuck anyway
So they're all right
Then a lot of people
Have been through things
And they haven't got to deal with it
So they're going through that thing
Of what people think
And always being the victim
Or the other way around
They're the bully because of it
That's the way they deal with it
Fight the world
Everyone's the enemy
Because of what they've been through
It can go either way.

TEDDY BEAR MAN

Is he carrying a baby
Or a teddy bear
It's a teddy bear
It looks like it could've been a baby
He's carrying it like a baby
There's some guy walking with a teddy bear
But he's holding it like it's a newborn
That's the way I would hold a new baby
I'm not sure he's nutty
I think he's just chosen to hold it that way
He keeps looking back
So I'm imagining his wife
Is going to turn the corner now
Pushing a pram or something
That's how it looks
But actually I'm having second thoughts
I think this guy
Is actually outside of his mind
I actually shouldn't be laughing
Because he's holding it like a newborn
And he's mumbling to himself
And he's looking around a bit lost
But now I'm thinking about it
It reminds me of a film I wrote

So I'm not going to laugh at it
Because it could be one of those
Postpartum situations that women have
I'm sure men have them as well
I'm not a psychologist but
I don't want to be laughing
At people's situations
Because he's holding it like a newborn
And he's kind of walking around with it
So I don't know
It could be someone that's lost a child
Or something
You never know
I won't be so quick to find it humorous
At first it was funny
Because I thought it was a child
And it turned out to be teddy bear
I was more laughing at myself
And then I realised
That he might not be too well
I was expecting a woman
To come behind him with a pram
But that didn't happen
And then I just saw him
Mumbling to himself
Holding this teddy bear

As if holding a baby
But he's not cradling it
Not that type of way
It's the way you'd create
A kind of human sling with your arms
And the baby's back would be to your chest
Facing away from you
So that's why I thought it was a baby
No-one holds a teddy bear like that
Is what I was thinking.

THE ENDING OF HUMANITY

I believe the world is on a decline
I believe it's ending bit by bit
Not the globe is going to blow up
Or the planet earth is going to blow up
But ending in terms of humanity
I feel our human-ness
And our humane humanity is declining
I feel like humanity is reduced a lot
And it's declining
More and more as time goes on
I really believe
Things like smartphones and technology
And this desire to have things now
And time being sped up
All these things that we accumulate
And design and use
To save time
And get things quicker
I feel that has taken some of the humanity
Away from us
We're losing patience
And that's part of our humanity
To be patient
We're losing that

Because everyone wants everything now
And fast
And computers
And now now now now now
We're just losing the ability
To sit down and have a conversation
Without being distracted
I feel that's how the world is ending
The world as in human
The human nature is ending
As we slowly go towards
Becoming androids and robots
The robots are taking over
And eventually
They'll kill all the humanity in us
Completely
Until we're just walking robots
And androids ourselves
Who used to be human
Or at least we still appear human
But we're not
There's no human element left
Because everything is operated digitally
And everything's at the touch of a button
The flick of a switch
Or they're activated by voice

No one will have time
For sitting down
And having conversations anymore
It's all about information now
How quick can I get the information
How quickly can I transfer the information
The human element was
When you asked somebody
How they're doing
You listened back to the response
There wasn't all of this distraction
In the middle
Where you don't even listen
To if they've actually answered the question
The person has already gone off
Into their next question
Before they listen to how you are
How are you?
And they're not even listening
To your answer
That's part of it
That's the human-ness dissolving
Or going away
No one's even listening to anyone anymore
It's all about processing information
The humanity is declining

The world is already ending
Someone asked me
When do I think the world is going to end
I said, not long now
Just a few more smartphones
At the dinner table
Because no one's really communicating
In the way we used to communicate
We're all now communicating
Through devices
We're together in a room
But we're all alone
Because we're all doing our own thing
Looking at our own little screens
In our own little world
Having our own little conversations
With other people
That are not in that room
Or if not actually physically doing that
Our mind is in those conversations
Or those interactions
With those other people
That are not in that room
That's what I mean by the world ending
The humanity
The humaneness of it

Is dissolving
It's going away
It's evaporating
I feel it's already ending
Who's to say there won't come a time
Where it ends completely
And it becomes something else
What will human beings evolve into
When there's no human
Or humane
Or humanity
Within anything.

THE FEAR OF A NEW RELATIONSHIP

The thought of all that hard work
Of meeting someone new
And going through the whole process
Of getting to know them again
And dating
And courting
If you've been with someone a little while
And you've gotten used to them
And their habits
All kind of stuff
And them to yours
The thought of meeting someone new
And exploring all of that again
And getting to know their habits
And their likes and dislikes
The whole journey is daunting
I can imagine
Why you'd stay with someone
You're really not into
Just because
You don't want to go through
The whole process
Of meeting someone
That you might not being into as well

Just the whole thought
Of dating from the beginning
After you've been in a long relationship
That's fucking scary
I can see why people stay together
Even though they're not completely happy
Or be on their own.

THE JOY OF SHORT TERM SACRIFICE

I'm not doing much
Just taking it easy
I'll be updating some stuff online
And that'll be it, man
I'm just taking it easy
Not doing too much
I'll meet up with a couple friends
For a little bit
Say hello
But I'm not going all out
Tomorrow I'll finish some tasks I had set
So I'm not going to be going too wild
And I'm cool
Because I'm just trying to finish
So I can be on to the next thing
It's like suffer now
And then have the glory later
It's just putting your head down
Head in the books and focusing
And then later on
You can have all the benefits
Making a few moves
That I can smile about later
I don't believe in

The whole work until you die thing
In some job you don't enjoy
Work
Retire
Sweating like a Hebrew slave
For very little pay
That's not the kind of hard work
I was talking about
I do believe in sacrifices
And giving up certain things
To achieve your goals
And suffering for a while
To actually enjoy life later
Not too much later of course
But after the hard work
I don't believe in working this job
That you hate
Just to have a lifestyle
To impress people
That you don't even like
It's not about that life for me.

THE OTHER WAY

I try not to be negative
Because negativity is just not it
When you have been around
So much negativity in life
You vow to be the other way
For me
I've been around a lot of it
With negativity
And being exposed to so much of it
It can go one of two ways
You can either
Go completely negative yourself
Because it has rubbed off on you
And you're now just a negative individual
Or it can go the other way
You choose to go the complete other way
Where you say, you know what
No, I'm not going that way
I'm going to be positive
And I am going to turn
Every negativity into a positive
Fortunately for me
I've also been exposed to a lot of positivity
Which counteracts the negativity

And fortunately it was enough
That it turned it on its head
And I'm completely the other way
That's just it
That's why people say
They find that I'm very positive
It's because I've gone the other way.

THE WAY IT HAS TO BE

I haven't got time
To watch all of this television
If I'm going to be making my own content
To the level that I want to
To the level that I aspire to
I can't watch everything that happens
If someone dies
I can't watch every single funeral
I can't watch everything
That Trump is doing
I can't watch every new movie
That comes out
I can't watch all the coverage on Brexit
And people's opinions on it
And every police story that happens
I just simply can't do it
If I plan to reach where I want to reach
In my own life and goals
And what I'm trying to do
It's just going to eat away
And eat away at the time
If I'm sitting there consuming
All of what the media put out
About whatever topic it might be

That's hot at the moment
It's just the way it has to be
And that means
I miss a lot of things
But at the same time
It means I make that time up
In creating
And putting out the content
I want to put out.

TRAVELLING THOUGHTS

What made me get to the point
Of not wanting to hold back on myself
And just being free and letting go
Travelling
Travelling did that for me
Travelling to all the countries
I travelled to recently
And having that space
To be inside my own head
Without distractions
Being away from the familiar things
Being away from my usual routine
We all have our own routine
Being away from all of that
And being able to process
Where I was
Sometimes when you're in something
You can't actually process where you are
And what's going on
Until you're outside of it
So being outside of it
Gave me the opportunity
To look at where I was
And where I wanted to go

Whether I was I happy there
Just travelling
Travelling did that
It just gave me a chance
To open up my mind
And just look out
Being on planes
Looking out the window
Just being able to think
And be in a space
Where I could collect my thoughts.

WEATHER REPORT

It's freezing, man
It's freezing
Zero degrees
I think it's like a hundred below
This is proper cold
I want the summer back
I heard definitely it's going to snow soon
I heard definitely
It doesn't mean it definitely is
But I definitely heard it
I definitely heard it's going to snow
I don't know
If it definitely is going to snow
I heard people talking about it
But I don't think they're weather people
And neither am I
So it might not snow
The sun might just come out.

WHAT UNDER THAT WEAVE DO?

I'm really not a fan of the weave thing
Because I don't like the idea
Of hair staying under there
And not washed for so long
It's like a woman gets a lace wig
How often is she's taking it off
I'm into hair quite a lot
Because I used to do hairdressing
But if I'm thinking about
Waking up to a woman every day
In that type of way
Then I'm not that keen on weave
I don't like that
I like to run my fingers
Through her scalp
It could be her hair or her scalp
I could do both at the same time
I like having the option
I don't like not knowing
If there's ants under there
Or mould
I don't like not knowing
Or maggots
So in terms of the woman

That I'm laying down with
Waking up next to
I'm not too great on weave
If a weave looks nice and cool
It's nice, it's good to look at
And you think, yes it looks good
But then I think
What's underneath there
That's what I think nowadays
I never used to think like that
I actually have a poem called
It's All About The Weave
I've been out with women
With all types of hair
Extensions and plaits
Locks and afro
Permed hair, relaxed hair
All different types
Every style you could probably think of
Weave wouldn't be top of my list
Wigs are fine, they're all right.

WHEN IN NEGATIVE SITUATIONS

I think to myself
What am I here to receive
Regardless of the outside elements
What am I here to gain
What have I come for
What do I want to leave with
It's almost like a military operation
We're going in
We've got to do this
And we've got to get out
We've come on a mission
I treat it a lot like that
I like to walk away
Feeling I got what I came for
Or something I wasn't expecting
But it made up for what I came for
It became the thing I came for
Sometimes you go into situations
And you get something you didn't expect
Like a person you meet
Who has got a contact for you
Or just a person you meet in general
Who just makes you feel good
Or a piece of information you receive

That was just worth your while being there
That was worth more than the money
There's always something I'm open to
What is it that I'm going to get out of this
That takes away
A lot of that stuff that can get to you
Or that negative stuff
When you go in there with that mindset
Like I'm here
I've come to receive something
That's going to make me better
I always go in with that mindset
It's some SAS type of thing
I've come in here on a mission
I've come to collect something
And I've got to get in and get out
It's like that whole sense of mission
It's a lot like that.

WHITE FACE FOR A DAY

If I could experience
Being of a different cultural background
For a day
I think I'd like to be white
Just to see what that side of life is like
Having a white face
Walking around
Experiencing life
Seeing if there are parallels
With things I experience being black
If I could definitely then
Put to rest some things
Or have to face some things
Depending on how my experience went
I'd be interested to see
What that would be like
Walking into establishments
Dressed the same way I dress
But obviously being a different colour
Seeing if I experience
The same things I experienced now
All of the things
All the positions I hold or don't hold
At this present time

And the ways I'm treated
In all different aspects of life
If they would have any difference
Based on me being in those environments
And situations
Being white
That I would be interested to see
Because obviously
The conversation on race
And black and white
And that whole thing
Is a lot
There's a lot of different things there
I would like to actually be in the shoes
Of a different self and different face
To see and experience how that is
And how I find it
Just to experience and see if I like it
And if I don't and why
And just to learn
It's all merely to learn
Just to see
Obviously it's only for a day
So I'm going to have to go back
But I'd find out as much as I can
Experience as much as I can

Achieve as much as I can
And just be more informed
And educated on something
That I'm looking at through a black face
I'll experience it from another side
I'd definitely enter into it
With an open mind
And experience it from outside of my bias
Outside of seeing just one side
Because I've never walked into
An establishment
Or been in a situation
Or been amongst people
Or anything
As a white person
So my whole experience
I feel
Maybe not all of it
But I believe some of it
Would be different
And that I would like to see
What the differences were
The parallels
All that stuff
So yeah
I'd be a white face for a day.

YOU CAN'T PLEASE EVERYBODY

I haven't seen her
What can I say
I put my hands up
She got annoyed with me
Because I had arranged to meet her
And I couldn't make it
And I hadn't let her know in good time
She's told me never to speak to her again
Well, not so much that
She just said goodbye
That I could have had the decency
To let her know kind of thing
And her last words were goodbye, Phoenix
I've obviously tried to apologise
And make amends
Asking her not to say goodbye
But I don't know how that's been received
I haven't heard back
It just didn't work out
Sometimes you just can't do
The best you want to do
So I haven't spoken to her
I haven't heard from her
I'm kind of giving her

A little time to cool off
I have this thing
Of agreeing to things
Because I want to be the good person
And I want to be agreeable
Yes, I'll be there
But it doesn't always work out
Because things happen
I do it with all good intentions
And then it just doesn't go to plan
I have to change plans
Then people get offended
Unfortunately
I don't do well with that
Because I don't like upsetting people
As much as I can help it
I like to be the guy that's seen to be
Making an effort
If he says he's going to be there
He's going to be there
He's going to come
I don't like to be the guy
Who has to break the plans
Or break the arrangements
I don't like being the bad guy in that sense
I don't do well with that

So that rendezvous didn't happen
I can only aim to do better in the future
I think for me
I'm going to have to be more ruthless
With my Yeses and my Nos
In terms of meeting people
And arranging dates
I'm trying to please everybody
And I'm trying to be available
Trying to not let anyone down
But I can't do it all
I'm just one person
Sometimes it just goes against me
I've realised I have to be more merciless
With my Yes and my No to things.

YOUR CREATIVITY WITHIN

You've got to get it out, man
It's got to come out
In some way, shape or form
Whether it's with a pad and pen
Or a pad and crayons
A piano
A dance floor
A stage
Or a camera
It's got to come out
Whether it's some pottery
Some sculpting
It's got to come out
It has to come out
It's in you
It's got to come out
In whatever form you choose
It's got to come out
That which is within you.

ABOUT THE AUTHOR

Phoenix James is an award winning Writer, Poet, Author and Spoken Word Recording Artist. He began performing his poetic words live on stages across the UK in 1998. His debut spoken word poetry album, *The A.R.T.I.S.T,* was released in 2000. His first limited edition printed collection of poetry, *To Whom It May Concern,* was published in 2003. He has toured and performed his poetry internationally since 2004. He has appeared in films, on television and radio shows, and collaborated with other artists, singer-songwriters, actors, musicians, filmmakers and producers. In 2013, he wrote, directed and produced the feature length mock documentary film, *Love Freely but Pay for Sex*. Phoenix James is the author of several poetry collections and has recorded and released several spoken word poetry albums including *Phenzwaan Now & Forever, A Patchwork Remedy for A Broken Melody, FREE, Haven for the Tormented, With All That Said,* and more than fifty spoken word poetry singles.

If you enjoyed reading this book, please leave a review online. The author reads every review and they help new readers discover his work.

PHOENIX JAMES

Photo by Phoenix James

Phoenix James lives in London, England.

Connect with Phoenix James on his online social media platforms via www.linktr.ee/ Phoenix_James and say you've read this book. To contact or learn more about Phoenix James and his creative journey or to receive updates via his Newsletter Mailing List, visit his official website at www.PhoenixJamesOfficial.com

Phoenix James Official